Walking
Auburn
Parks

A Local Photographic Journey

by

Deborah Taylor-Hough

Walking
Auburn
Parks

About This Book

This photographic journey was inspired by course readings from the Master of Fine Arts in Creative Writing and Poetics program at the University of Washington Bothell.

Primary inspirational texts/resources:

> *An Attempt at Exhausting a Place in Paris* by Georges Perec
> *Sixty Morning Walks* by Andy Fitch
> *Midwinter Day* by Bernadette Mayer
> *Camera Lucida* by Roland Barthes
> *Urban Tumbleweed: A Tanka Diary* by Harryette Mullen
> The photographic walks of Richard Long

Contents

Walk #1
Roegner Park

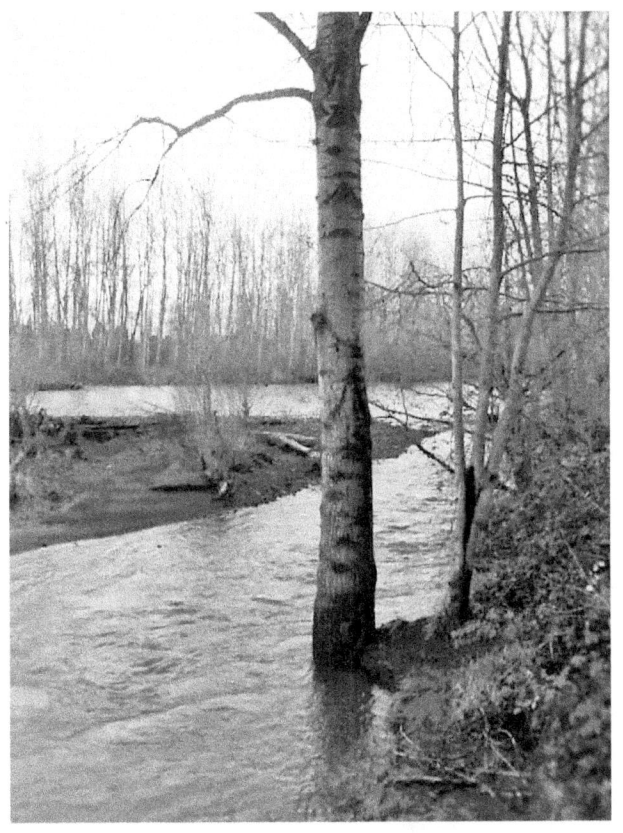

Walking Roegner Park
Auburn, WA – January 16th – 8:15am

There's only one other car in the parking lot right now. Guess it'll be an empty, quiet morning. Which trail to choose? The dirt path or the concrete one? The dirt's closer to the river with a better view. So I guess a left turn, it is. The trail's still soggy from last night's heavy rainstorm. Chilly. Definitely wouldn't want to fall into the White River in January.

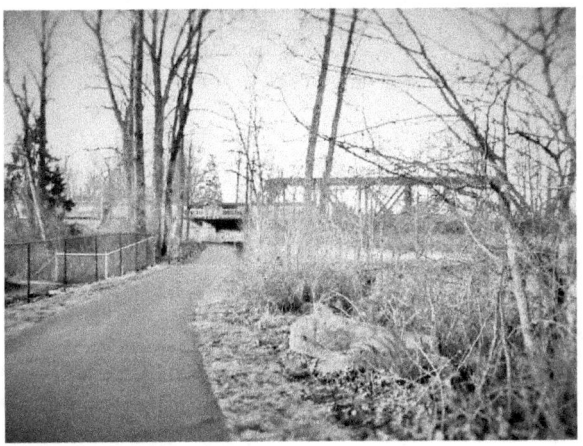

I listen as I walk. The sounds of crows in the trees. The river. My own quiet footfalls. There are two other people in the park now, talking beneath a broken picnic shelter. They look like high school students waiting for morning classes to begin. The shelter's encircled with bright yellow Caution tape. I guess a cautionary warning won't scare off teenage lovebirds seeking some "alone" time. Feel a little like I'm intruding. Heading on.

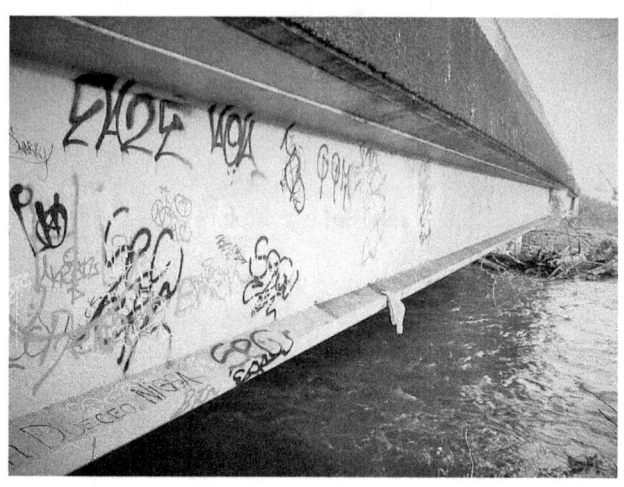

Choose the river path
Sound of crows, footfalls, river
Soggy from night's rain
The wind is quiet today
Grasses bent from prior storms

Across the river, I can just barely see the tops of several mobile homes. The homes usually aren't visible when the leaves are on the trees. Living so close to the river, heavy rains sometimes bring floods to their neighborhood.

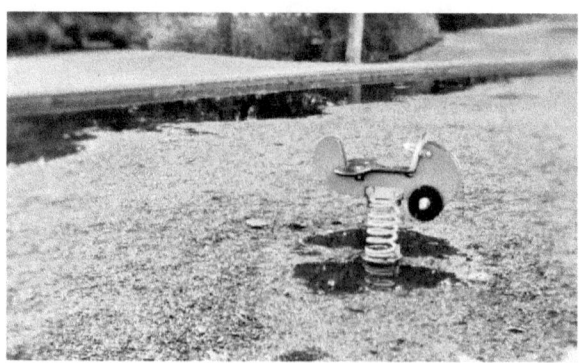

The air is so still. So quiet. Tall grasses beside the path lean over, pointing to the northwest from an earlier wind. Actually, that's a little odd. Usually the wind in Auburn comes from the southwest. Yes, I pay attention to these things.

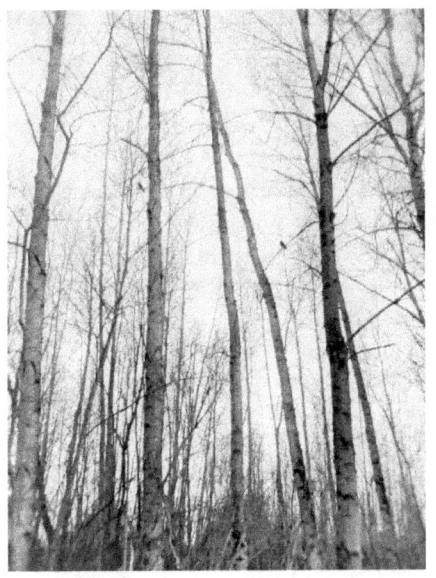

Should I take the muddy side trail that leads through the damp woods? No, I think not. Vanity wins and I decide to protect my new shoes. A haunting voice seems to whisper that the path less traveled would make all the difference. Hush, Robert Frost.

> *Sun barely risen*
> *Empty, cold I start to walk*
> *Well-trodden concrete*
> *Right or left, is the question,*
> *To take the trail less traveled?*

Quite a few more crows coming out. They're scolding me loudly as I walk. Are they following me? It's hard to tell if it's the same crows, or if they're passing their scolding off to their family and friends down the line.

Listening again, I hear a distant train whistle. The sounds of cars on A Street. The river rushing. The crows. My footfalls. There's a long train heading over the bridge. I can't even see the end of it. The graffiti on the railroad bridge is a gentle reminder that this is an urban city park.

There's a large backhoe parked by the street. My kids loved visiting Auburn's Public Works department on Kids' Day. Sitting in the cabs of the big "scoopers" and working the controls was something they looked forward to every year. Do kids still climb in the trucks and backhoes on Kids' Day?

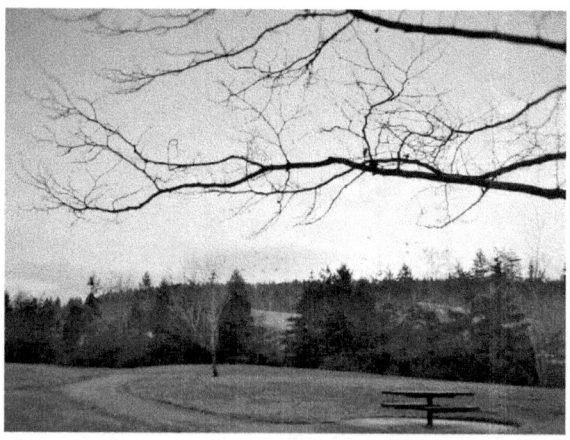

I've reached the trail's end. The Auburn Valley Humane Society isn't open yet—not until 10—but I can see volunteers inside cleaning cages, emptying litterboxes, refilling food dishes, walking dogs. Two friendly pit bulls look out longingly at me. Hello, sweet babies. Several cats are thoroughly engrossed while they intensely watch the workers bringing their food. Breakfast time, kitties.

Heading back to the park, I see a small sign about wetlands near the concrete trail, telling visitors how wetlands in the city are important to help offset the pavement and all the other impervious surfaces. The signage is essentially a trailside public service announcement.

Behind some bushes, I can just barely see a small pond with a pair of mallards. The sun's beginning to peek over the hillside. Next to the trail, there are a number of fluffy snowberry plants. Someone once told me that if you step on the berries, they'll pop. But not today. I tried it. Squish. I guess they're too wet to pop. Now I think it looks like a flat albino cranberry.

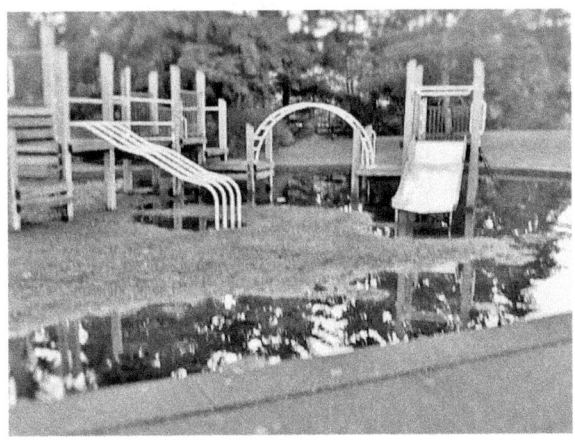

The sunshine's moving quickly, already reaching the tops of the taller trees. As more sun becomes visible, I see and hear more birds. Not just the crows now, but many smaller birds, too. Sparrows, chickadees, finches. Wow! Startled by a flock of flickers! There's even a pilated woodpecker hopping up and down the trunk of a tree while Canada geese honk noisily overhead.

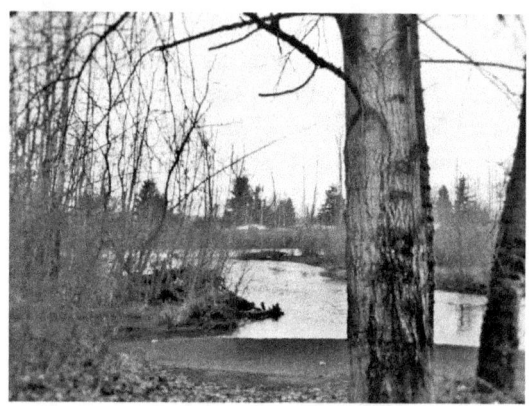

The trail's still empty. The play equipment sits abandoned in the midst of a large puddle. I see reflections of the sky. Oops. I just got a little too close to the mud and it sucked on my new shoes. Turned around quickly, but left footprints in the muck.

Playing detectives
Lots of mem'ries at this park
Kids playing 'gators
Stop! Don't touch the hot lava!
Nearly twenty years ago

There's a rail for tying up horses. Do people actually ride horses here? I don't think I've ever seen a horse at the park. Or even their droppings.

I think the tree's bark looks like a jigsaw puzzle. The park is beginning to awaken. Workers arrive and open the restrooms. They stop for a moment to eye me curiously as I'm taking random photos. Guess it's a little early for photos.

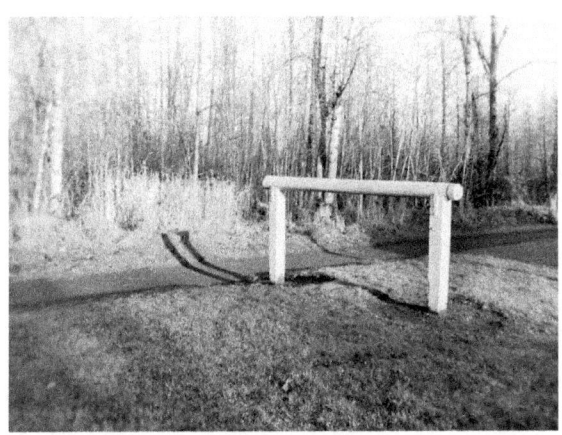

The sun's fully up now, and the dog walkers are arriving and unloading themselves and their furry walking partners in the parking lot. They all head off to the off-leash play area. I can see a German shepherd and a very happy terrier.

Time to go home.

Walk #2
Les Gove Community Park

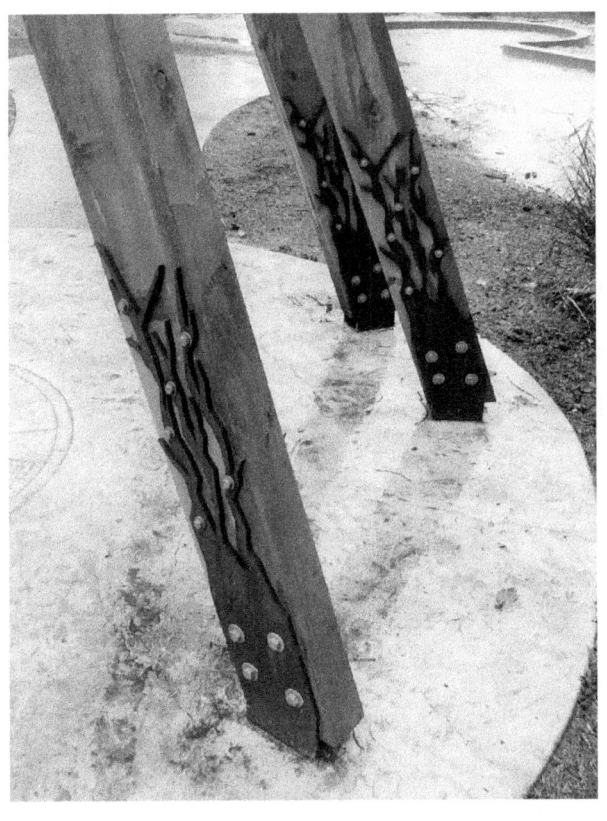

Walking Les Gove Community Park

Auburn, WA – January 17th – 12:45pm

Today I planned to take another early morning walk.

But … rain.

I waited and waited for the storm to ease up. But it didn't. Reluctantly, I removed the purring cat from my lap, put on my raincoat, and bucked up.

I parked near the water play area. The park is lonely in the rain. Deserted. Only one person nearby, and they're pacing frantically outside the porta-potty.

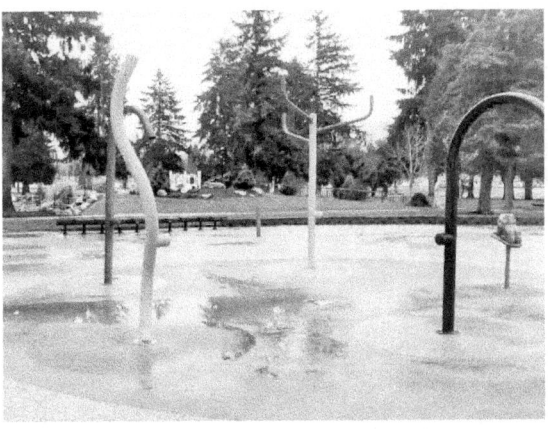

Another day's walk full of memories. We lived a block from Les Gove. Now there are new play structures. The new playground appears to be safe, educational, artistically designed, and probably a whole lot of fun. Auburn's actually a good place to be a child.

Bikes on training wheels
More memories of childhoods
Sliding and swinging
Learning to do monkey bars
Crackers and nuts for the squirrels

Back in the days when I had three kids, a double-stroller, and a bike with training wheels, the main play equipment here was just a simple wooden structure. Now it's off to the side, barely even noticed. Forgotten. My kids learned to do the Monkey Bars here. This was also their introduction to slides and tire swings.

Finally, the rain eases somewhat. I'm still glad for my raincoat, thought. A small group of disheveled men huddle under the trees. I suspect they're trying to keep dry. Several of them eye me a bit suspiciously was I'm taking pictures. Are they worried about photos of their activities? I probably don't even want to know what they're doing.

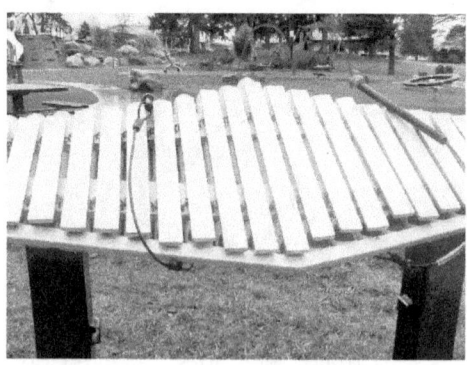

A grey squirrel runs by, but stops momentarily to beg. Sorry little fella. I don't have anything for you today. It scurries up a tree.

Everything is quiet. No bird sounds. Not even crows. I see a few seagulls at other end of park, quietly feeding in the grass. I can hear the sound of rain falling lightly on my raincoat's hood.

I stop and attempt to play Do-Re-Mi on the play area's xylophone. Evidently it isn't tuned for that particular song. Lovely tones, though. Anything I play sounds beautiful. Even musical nonsense. A man on the trail across the way stops and listens to my rainy concert for a moment. Suddenly I feel self-conscious and embarrassed. I stop playing. Funny how for small children, having an audience usually increases the pleasure of playing. That childlike fearlessness somehow gets lost as we age and become aware of others' judgments.

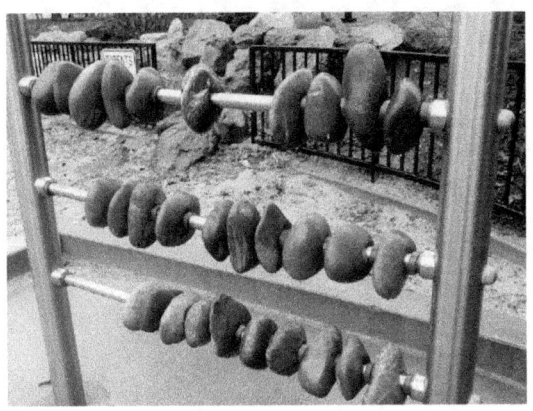

Back on the trail, a woman passes. She nods and smiles. Glancing at the rain, she says, "Nice day for ducks."

Rain. Raining. Raincoat.
Rainy January day
A good day for ducks
Alone. Not really lonely.
Water sliding down the cheek

A twenty-something couple with a blonde dog pass by. The dog is sweet and wants to give out kisses. But his people say, "NO! Heal!" No doggie kisses for me today.

When my kids were young, this hill was gigantic and difficult to walk up or down without tipping. Rolling, laughing, grass stains, dandelion tufts, mussed hair. Treasured memories. Seemed those days would last forever.

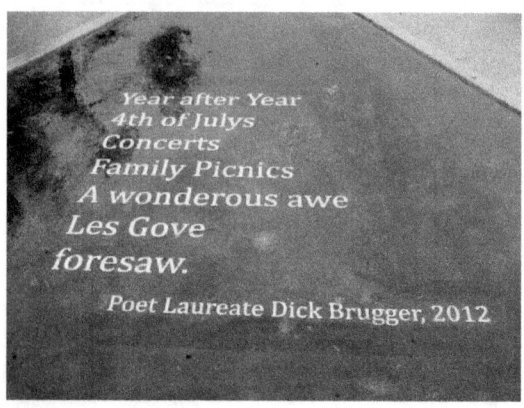

Year after Year
4th of Julys
Concerts
Family Picnics
A wonderous awe
Les Gove
foresaw.

Poet Laureate Dick Brugger, 2012

Auburn has a Poet Laureate? Who knew?

> *Library warm. Dry.*
> *Homeless stay close to this park*
> *Soccer moms and kids*
> *Poverty mixed with plenty*
> *Free hot lunches in summer*

Two teens pass by on skateboards. One is being pulled along, sled dog style, by an energetic Border collie.

I wonder what's on display at the White River Historical Museum? There's so much history in Auburn. There's a lot of newness, too. Even a new library. It was always nice when we lived around the corner from the library with young kids and no car. I never felt stranded. The park, the library, the wading pool, ice cream cones at Big Daddy's, were all just an easy walk away.

Big Daddy's restaurant is closed. I have lots of tasty memories of eating their soft-serve vanilla ice cream cones on hot summer days. This area where the spray park is now used to be a wading pool. Our family spent many happy afternoons splashing in the pool. I wonder which is more fun from a kid's perspective? Pretending to swim in the wading pool or playing with the new spray fountains?

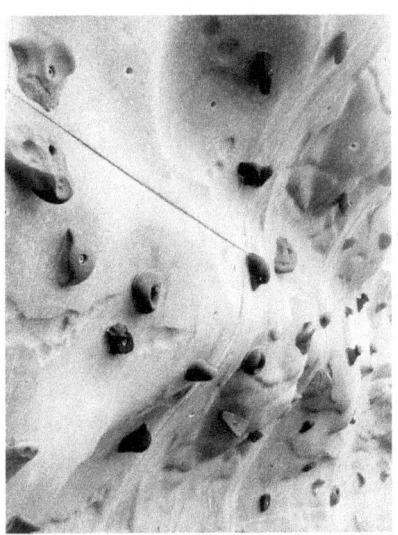

I've completed the circle, and am just about to step into my car when I hear a distinctive "chick-a-dee-dee-dee" overhead in a tree. Can't see the birds, but it's nice to know the chickadees are around. It was a quiet, peaceful walk today.

Rainy days are good walking days.

Walk #3
Game Farm Park

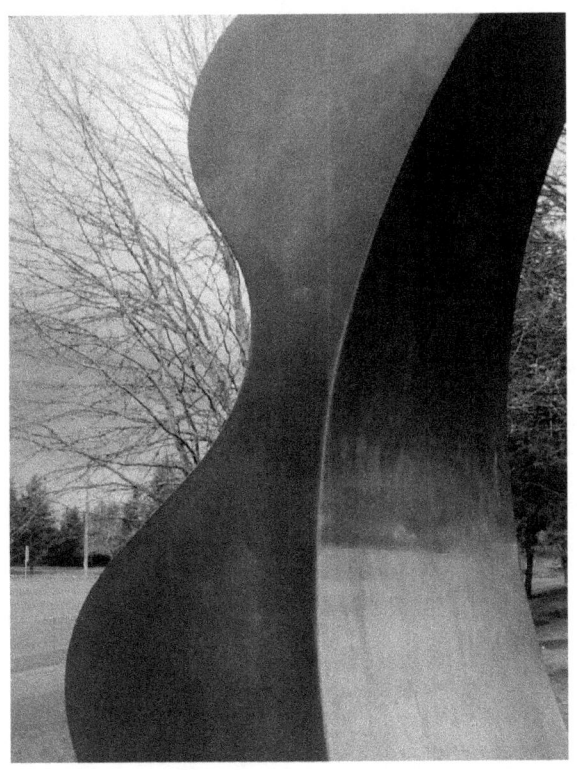

Walking Game Farm Park
Auburn, WA – January 18th – 1:00pm

Headed out the door intending to a North Auburn park, but skies that direction are black with clouds. South Auburn seems sunny. Pick Game Farm to stay dry.

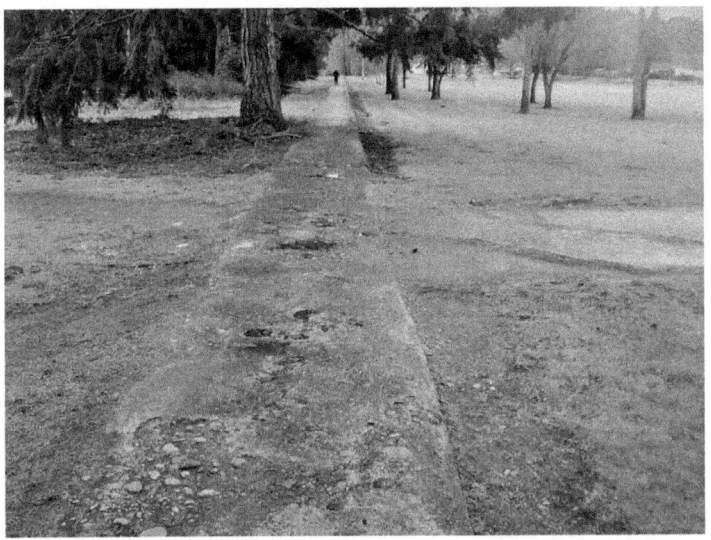

Occasional sun breaks. People not from Seattle don't say "sun breaks." What do they call it? Park is fairly empty. Out walking during the Seahawks game.

Soccer game on the field. A quiet crow watches from the grass. Several teenage girls squeal loudly. They're trying to touch a squirrel. Every time they get close, they squeal. Scare the squirrel away.

Walk past the amphitheater. Remember church services there on summer Sundays. A garbage can overturned in the wet grass at top of seating area. Squirrel runs up. Stops to beg. Staring hopefully. Runs up a tree before photo.

Crows. A few seagulls. More squirrels. Sounds of the river. A whistle blowing from the soccer game. A scolding crow.

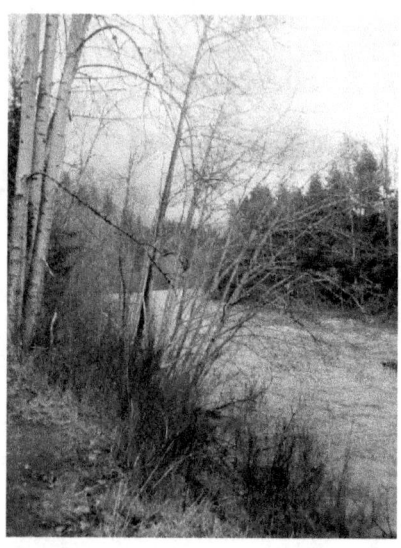

Choose to walk by river. Running high, murky, brown. Trail is rocky but dry. Walk on concrete wall by grassy area. Anyone else walking today? Squirrel girls are trying to find a tree to climb. All branches too high off ground.

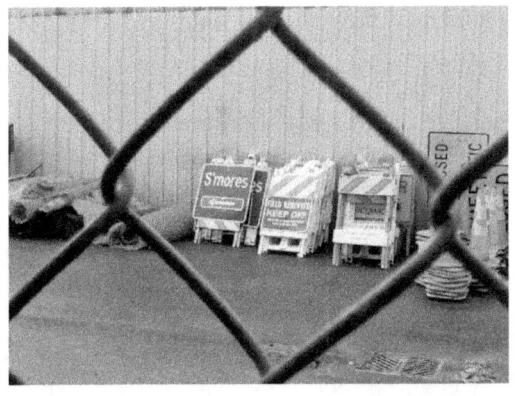

Another solitary person in distance walking on concrete wall, too. Can't tell from here which way they're heading. Almost a shadow person from this distance.

Sign points to the left and says, "S'mores." Reached top of hill, clouds parted, standing in sunshine. For a moment. A brief bit of blue.

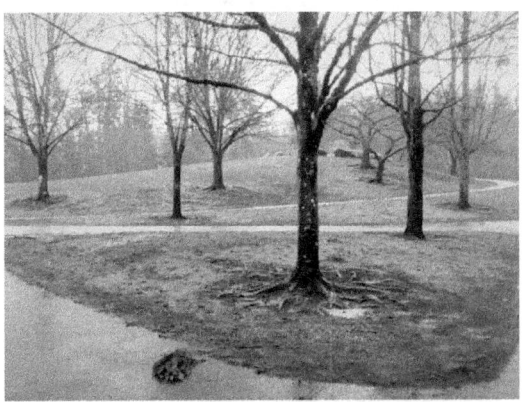

Sit on a boulder. Remember kids playing on this hill. A hot summer day. Sledding down grassy hillside on blocks of ice. Great way to cool off. Hill seemed big then. Now looks small.

A recurring theme—big hills in memory become small hills when viewed today.

Dark clouds coming this way. Ominous. Not sure how quickly the clouds are moving. Zip raincoat. Stop by the Sun Circle sculpture. So many family photos sitting in the middle of this. Sunny days, cloudy days, spring days, fall days, summer days. And now today. No kids today. A cold, empty sculpture.

Rain's starting. Quickly pull up jacket's hood. Now hail falling. Heavier and heavier. Bouncing off grass and concrete path. Bouncing off hood. Getting bigger. Falling harder. Stings. It hits hood, jacket, hands, face.
Older gentlemen takes cover by restrooms. Join him under shelter. Laugh together. "Totally didn't expect that! Didn't even see it comin'!"

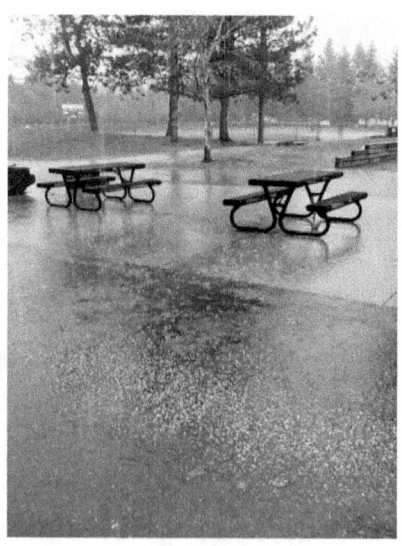

"BOOM!" Thunder. Eyes wide. More laughter. Weather falling hard. Three girls come running. One skips, "This is so cool! It's so fun! I can't feel my face! It's so cold!" Second runs by. "Omigosh, it's COLD!" Third, lags behind. Whispers. "I want my Mommy."

"BOOM!" Third child screams. "I don't wanna die!" Ducks under eaves with friends, older gentleman, and lone walker. Timid one looks at others. No fear. Nervous smile. Joins laughter. Two men run past. Laughing in hailstorm. Two white puppies run happily behind. Everyone's laughing.

Hail stops. Rain subsides. Smiles all around. Time to disband little makeshift group. Head back out from under shelter of restroom doorway. Girls find puddles to splash in. Lone walker finds puddles to photograph.
Older gentlemen heads back home. Watch the rest of the game. "They were behind 16 to nothing. Maybe the Hawks will come back in the second half."

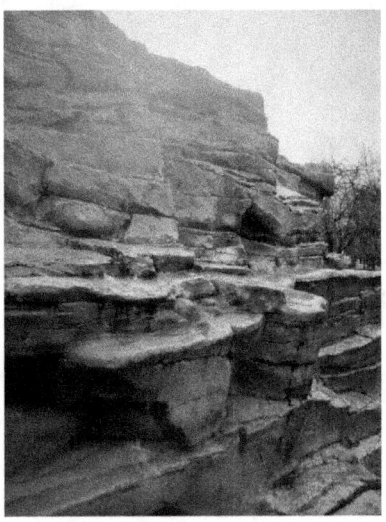

Heading toward the car. Notice new playground equipment. A rock wall. A slide. Need to duck underneath slide when another rainstorm hits. Shelter isn't working. Keep walking. Now know raincoat is water-resistant, not water-proof. Not a dry inch left on icy body. Hailstorm rain is cold.

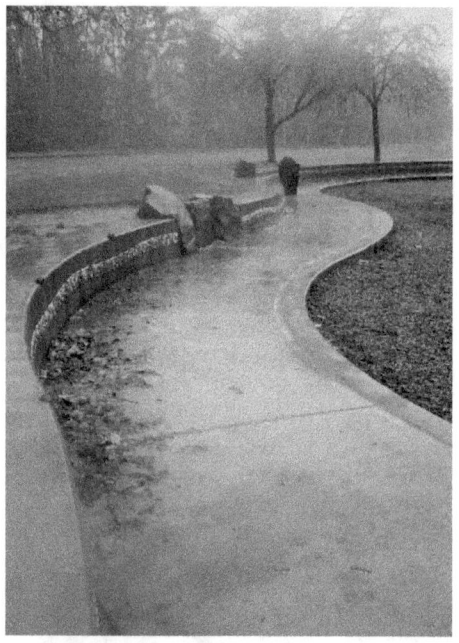

Camera lens getting wet, fogging up. Even when hidden deeply in coat sleeve. Warm bowl of soup, hot shower, dry clothes await at home.

Walk #4
Isaac Evans Park

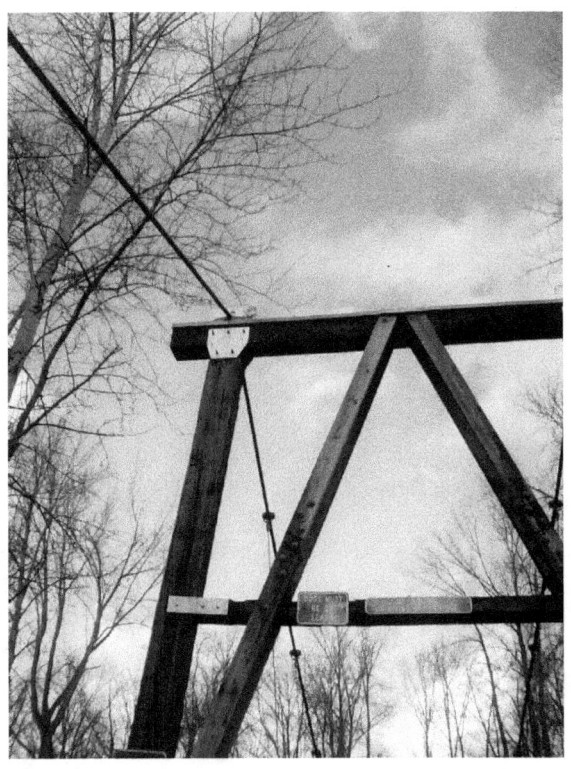

Walking Isaac Evans Park

Auburn, WA – January 19th – 1:15pm

Parked by bridge. First thing seen were finches. Lots and lots
of finches. A full flock of finches. Guess this is a part of
Auburn where finches live. Haven't seen many on earlier
walks.

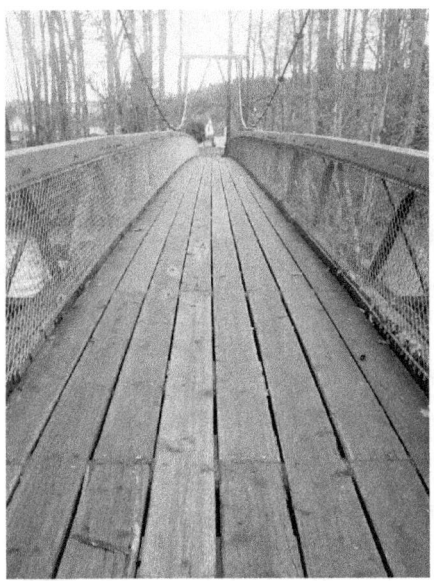

Bushes by roadside alive with hopping, chattering birds.
Sunshine. A gaggle of geese lying in the grass, enjoying sun.
Someone put up a Little Library here several years ago. Never
seem to be books in it.

Love this suspension bridge. Something industrial about it.
Chain link fencing. Giant bolts. Thick twisted wire ropes.
Both picturesque and raw. Like this neighborhood. Rougher

than some of the other neighborhoods, flanking the Green River.

Cross the bridge. Greeted by wildlife. A flock of Juncos, squirrels, crows. The animals scatter as lone walker approaches; regroup again as soon as coast is clear.

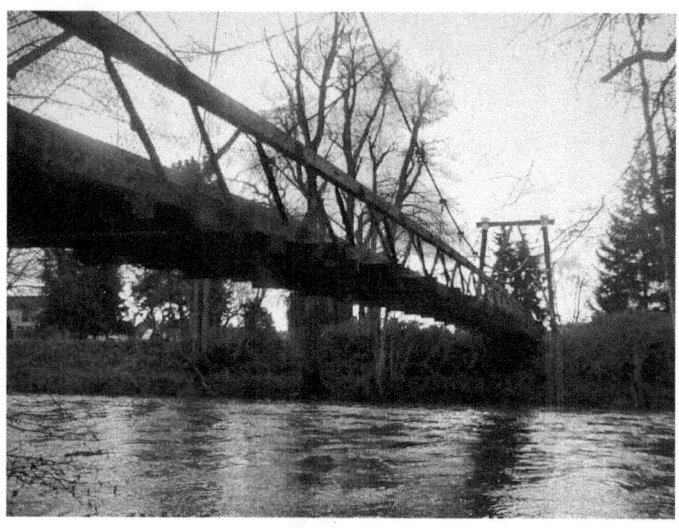

Detour down by riverside. Looks cold. Glad sun's shining. Only sounds—the river flowing quietly, occasional cars going by on other side of bushes.

Cracks in sidewalk everywhere from tree roots. Nature wins out.

Lots to see now. Crows. Trees. Bushes. Litter. Cars. Houses. River. Apartments. Tree stumps. Grass. Split-rail fence. Squirrel. Leaves. Twigs. Puddles.

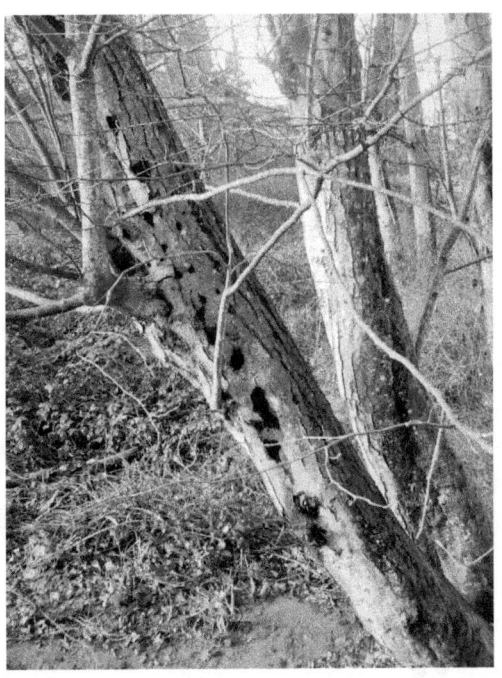

Wander over by river again. Footprints and paw prints in sand. Look back to see what sort of tracks shoes left. Can hardly tell where stepped. Slight disappointment.

Another play structure the kids grew up with. Stop to make art in the gravel. Drag large stick in gravel and make designs. Young family coming. Don't want to intrude on their family time.

More art in the park. On the outside restroom wall. Avidly dressed Seahawks fans walk past. Enjoy this park. But return trip is essentially same walk, just in reverse. Don't notice anything new or different.

A dog and owner. Another pit bull. Seen more pit bulls while walking this week than any other breed. Hadn't realized how popular they were in Auburn.

Walking. Walking more. Same trail. Same crows. Same squirrels in same places. Last half of walk is one long déjà vu.

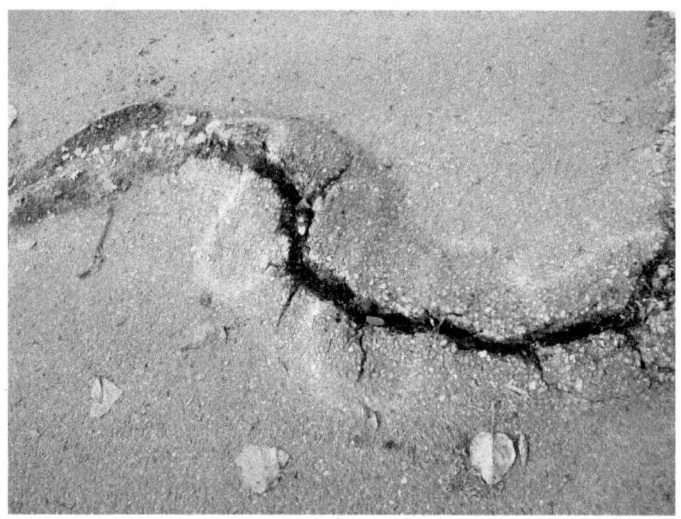

Man and dog walk past on bridge. Chat briefly. Dog gives kisses. "He's so deprived and starved for attention. Nobody ever pets him, you'd think from how he acts." Laughter.

Today is MLK, Jr. Day. Should do something to contribute to community today. Passing Little Library again. Remember some books in car for friend's son.

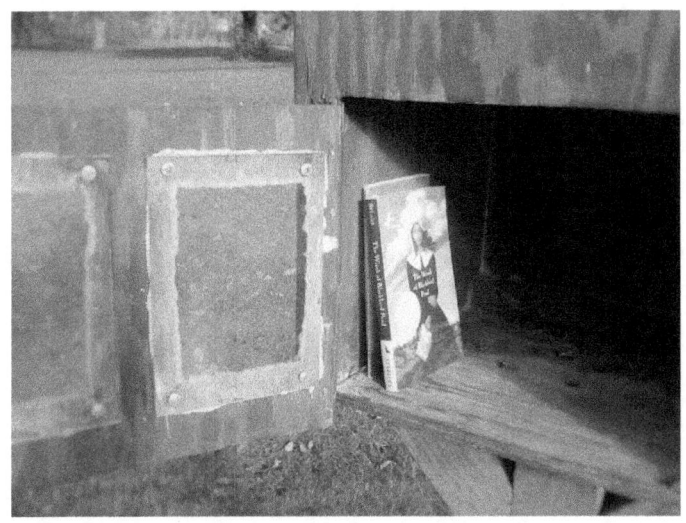

Look through book bag. *The Witch of Blackbird Pond.* Not sure friend's son would enjoy it. Leave book in Little Library instead. Decide to gift the community today with literature.

Will look for more books at home. Hope to fill the Little Library.

Author's Statement

Reflections on Walking Literature and a Sense of Place

Taking leisurely walks in local parks has been a regular occurrence in my life for many years. But writing about those walks and chronicling my thoughts and experiences? Not so much. Experimenting with keeping a visual record of several walks with my cell phone's tiny camera and then documenting those walks in prose and poetry was surprisingly time-consuming, but beneficial and personally rewarding.

The experience led me to contemplate several different literary topics I was previously unaware of or hadn't explored in any depth. Those topics include walking literature, quotidian literature, photography in literature, observing the natural world, and various literary formats—poetry, prose, visual, etc.—that can be used to express those topics.

My recent contemplations have led me to a variety of far-flung spots including Walden Pond with Henry David Thoreau, a street in Paris with Georges Perec, several neighborhoods in New York City with Andy Fitch, a variety of city parks in Los Angeles with Harryette Mullen, and the post office, library, and Main Street shops in Lenox, Massachusetts with Bernadette Mayer. A strong sense of place is a common component of walking literature.

While researching, I explored books and topics covered in both MFA classes this quarter that I have found to be applicable to my own series of Walks in some way. I looked at a variety of ways I can apply the ideas to my own developing poetic about walking around my hometown. I was curious about creative ways I can format my local walks or explorations around town, and how else might I approach an in-depth examination of Auburn, Washington through various literary devices.

Walking literature has a long history. Henry David Thoreau was an early American proponent of using walking as an inspiration for writing and creativity. Thoreau's essay, "Walking," was one of his last writings and actually published after his death. If I were to add a subtitle to his essay, it would be, "Sauntering Towards the Holy Land." Thoreau talks about walking as "sauntering" based on the original use of the word as it referred to religious pilgrimages or crusades.[1] He took his walking/sauntering seriously, and said,

> If you are ready to leave father and mother, and brother and sister, and wife and child and friends, and never see them again—if you have paid your debts, and made your will, and settled all your affairs, and are a free man—then you are ready for a walk.[2]

I felt while reading this essay that "Walking" was an analogy of his life and a reflection on his impending death—thus sauntering towards the Holy Land takes on the double meaning of both Nature and Heaven. Thoreau believed that in order to preserve his health and spirit, he needed to spend at least four hours a day outdoors, and he thought people should "walk like camels," ruminating on their thoughts as they sauntered. It was important to keep a mindful awareness as a person walked and to be aware of when the exterior world becomes in tune with the interior thought-life.

Ben Jacks states that "the bodily experience of walking and the pace of engagement with the world opens the space to recognize its beauty and distress."[3] Thoreau walked in the countryside surrounded by fields and woods, but

---

[1] Thoreau, Henry David. *Walking*. Page 1

[2] Ibid.

[3] Jacks, Ben. "Reimagining Walking: Four Practices." *Journal of Architectural Education* (1984-) 57.3 (2004). Page 9.

walking and ruminating isn't only limited to walks taken in the wilderness. Bernadette Mayer, Andy Fitch, and Harryette Mullen have all spent time walking in small towns, large cities, urban parks, and then using those walks as literary fuel for their writing practices. Francis Alys states,

> Walking, in particular drifting, or strolling, is already—within the speed culture of our time—a kind of resistance. Paradoxically, it's also the last private space, space from the phone or email. But it also happens to be a very immediate method for unfolding stories. … The walk is simultaneously the material of the artistic transaction. And the city always offers the perfect setting for accidents to happen.[4]

Combining walking around her hometown with the small everyday details of her family life, Bernadette Mayer successfully combined the practices of walking, poetry, and quotidian observations. Referring to the quotidian practices of Wallace Stevens, Siobhan Phillips states that

> [T]he poet evinces a modern citizen's vision of the common as well as a modern artist's choice of the commonplace; his use of the quotidian allows a seemingly esoteric craft to join, elucidate, and celebrate democratic life."[5]

Likewise, Mayer's poetic work elucidates and celebrates the quotidian. While reading *Midwinter Day* by

---

[4] Alys, Francis. "Interview" (with Russell Ferguson), *Francis Alys*, ed. Cuauhtemoc Medina. London: Phaidon, 2007. Page 31.
[5] Phillips, Siobhan. "Wallace Stevens and the Mode of the Ordinary." *Twentieth Century Literature* 4.1 (Spring 2008). Page 1.

Bernadette Mayer, I was struck by how familiar she is with her local landscape. The streets, businesses, people, and history of Lenox, Massachusetts all found their way into Mayer's examination of a single day in her life as a mother, a writer, and a resident of Lenox.

Before Mayer even leaves her apartment, we're introduced to several of her neighbors—the hairdressers downstairs, the gay couple next door, the mail-order baker, the child psychologist—and given a quick historical tour of her building, which she tells us is "a three-story turn-of-the-century red brick apartment house where rich men's coachmen used to live with their families in the thirties."[6]

As Mayer leaves home and ventures out for her walk around town, she reminds me of a chatty and reflective tour guide who intersperses historical tidbits with personal stories and memories.

Lenox

Used to be called Yokuntown after Chief Yokun,
A Mahican of the River Tribe who lived by the Hudson
In good weather they hunted in the Berkshires,
Not fools enough to live here what they call year-round
Charles Lenox was the third Duke of Richmond
Great Grandson of King Charles II
                Now the town's rich people
Live on Yokun Avenue near the private country club.[7]

---

[6] Mayer, Bernadette. *Midwinter Day*. New York, NY: New Directions Corporation, 1999. Page 35.

[7] Mayer, 42.

I can see how Mayer must have done quite a bit of research prior to writing her epic one-day poem in order to include the historical details she provides.

When Part Three of *Midwinter Day* begins, the layout of the page changes and takes on more of the look of a traditional poem. Phrases. Short thoughts. Quick observations. Down the stairs, out into the weather. Mayer shares with readers about the snow, the people, and her ever-present history lessons.

> The dark brown stairs
> Towards the doors
> Of this house
>   Wisdom's gray sky remembers
> Snow is white crystals
> Hall mirror,
> Misaligned and broke strollers,
>   Sex and going out
> What there is of snow icing
> The path plowed over the ground[8]

Mayer's list of famous people from Lenox reads like a Who's Who of American letters:

> Nearby are the former homes
> Of Edith Wharton, Nathaniel Hawthorne, Herman Melville,
> William Cullen Bryant and Edith Wharton's mother-in-law,
> The birthplace of W. E. B. DuBois,
> And places Oliver Wendell Holmes frequented.[9]

---

[8] Mayer, 41
[9] Mayer, 42.

Mayer walks down the street, visits the post office, and then stops to observe the signs, handbills, and stickers by the front of the local library. She observes the library patrons, lists the books she and her children are borrowing this day, and then launches into the now infamous description of Marie, her daughter's, tantrum.

> Marie Maria Callus is having a tantrum in the library
> She won't surrender her books, she won't put on her coat
> It's a violent willful outburst of rage and annoyance …
> She is hard and soft at once, hot and suddenly cool, mad,
> … she is fiery and dark, nothing tempers it,
> …
> She has the strength of a thousand women and men, …
> The veins in her neck bulge with rage, rapid and combust[10]

The dreaded public tantrum—a simple, everyday event in the life of parents everywhere—takes on the proportions of an epic Wagnerian opera in Mayer's capable hands. Marie seems to be almost a Titan in her small coat with those childhood books held tightly in her intensely contrary grasp.

While reading *Midwinter Day*, I found myself drawn to Mayer's depictions of neighbors and random passersby. She encapsulates some of her observations about the people which tells the reader that the community is made up a variety of people, classes, and ages. A hint of personal judgement creeps in at this point, too.

---

[10] **Mayer, 44.**

[T]he community of local people
Some of whom are limited, bigoted, stodgy or mean
Others among them love nature, and certain kinds of
art
And a man we know who lives alone here says he's
lonely
He just reads, drinks, keeps a journal and sniffs
cocaine
The town adolescents shout and skid around in their
cars
And leave half-empty bottles of Jack Daniels in the
park.
The high school imported a black man from Harlem
to play on
Their championship basketball team, the Lenox
Millionaires
And the rumor is the schools are so bad the students
Don't always learn to really read and write in
sentences.[11]

This last part seems almost like a comment on how far the town has fallen from its literary roots of Hawthorne and DuBois. I wonder what the people of Lenox think about her generalizations of some of their town's people being "limited, bigoted, stodgy or mean" and users of cocaine and Jack Daniels? Does Mayer even care what the community thinks? Mayer asks, "But why do we live here?"[12] as if she isn't certain, herself, what the attractions are to living in this particular small town with all its quirks, charming and otherwise.

While Mayer's sense of place was firmly set in the streets and shops of Lenox, Georges Perec created a strong

---

[11] Mayer, 45.
[12] Ibid.

sense of place in his book, *An Attempt at Exhausting a Place in Paris*. He wasn't walking through the streets, however, like Mayer had done with her children. Perec placed himself in a series of stationary spots around Tabac Saint-Suplice in Paris where he spent three days carefully observing "what happens when nothing happens other than the weather, people, cars, and clouds."[13] He begins his observations on Day One by simply cataloging what he sees: The content of signs (letters, symbols, numbers, slogans), the varieties of ground coverings in the square (asphalt, compact sand and gravel, stone), living things (trees, pigeons, dogs, humans), food (lettuce, bread, cake), bus schedules, colors, and tourists.[14] In his second entry, Perec begins to offer more observations of the people he sees: Conversations, means of movement, styles of walking, body positions. By returning to the same place for a second time that day, he seems to be recognizing some of the rhythms of the people and the traffic. The recurring bus routes almost beat time, "A 96 passes by. An 87 passes by. An 86 passes by. A 70 passes by. A 'Grenelle Interlinge' truck passes by. Lull. There is no one at the bus stop. A 63 passes by. A 96 passes by."[15] The fact that Perec notices the lull indicates he's becoming familiar with the comings and goings of the busses. By his second day of observations, he begins by looking for differences from his earlier visits. He loses interest in the busses. He focuses more during the last two days on the people, the pigeons, the children, the church events, and the life being lived out in front of him.

Through her memories and stream of consciousness ramblings as she took a single walk on a single day, Mayer was able to show the reader that she was well-acquainted with

---

[13] Perec, Georges, and trans. Marc Lowenthal. *An Attempt at Exhausting a Place in Paris*. Cambridge, MA: Wakefield, 2010. Page 3.
[14] Perec, 5.
[15] Perec, 11.

Lenox, its history, and its people. Her knowledge and sense of place comes from her past history with the community. She isn't furthering her knowledge of Lenox through her observations, but using her observations to share her knowledge with others. Perec, however, took a different approach. Through his sequence of visits to the same spot, the reader experiences what feels like a present-tense "coming-to-know" a place. The reader doesn't get a sense that Perec has a strong history with this particular square in Paris, but gains more of a sense that Perec is gaining his first real observations of this square. Mayer's observations were present tense, but she used her current observations to evoke the past and the history of the place where she was walking. Perec's observations were also present tense, but he used his observations to evoke the current flow of life as it passed through his view. Mayer physically passed through the town as she observed it, while Perec allowed the town to pass through his line of sight as he remained stationary. Mayer put meaning—both personal and historical—into her observations, while Perec was grappling with "what he termed the 'infraordinary': the markings and manifestations of the everyday that consistently escape our attention as they compose the essence of our lives."[16]

Thoughts on Applications to My Own Walks

Thoreau worried that a time would come when there would be very little wilderness left, and that the wild lands would be fenced off into private property, thus making walkers/saunters into trespassers. I believe we're now living in that "evil day" he predicted—the time of fenced off acreage and never-ending "No Trespassing" signs is upon us. City parks are the closest thing to wilderness for the city dweller. Auburn even has a park called Wilderness Park

[16] Perec, 51.

which sounds lovely and wild, but has a Frisbee golf course running through the entire park, making for a dangerous saunter for the casual walker. Rather than feeling refreshed by a wild experience at the Wilderness Park, I often come home a little more stressed than when I left. Continually checking for flying discs coming out of the woods is a bit anxiety-provoking.

As Thoreau recommends, I think I do tend to ruminate when I walk, especially when I walk alone, but I have discovered through my recent walking adventures and writing experiments that I previously tended to forget what I'd thought about, and then would just go on with my day after the walk. Now that I am making a point to remember where my daydreams take me, and to keep a written record of my thoughts, the time I spend walking has become more meaningful to me.

While my children were small, I lived in Auburn for eight years, moved away for ten years, and then came back to Auburn for the past ten years. Auburn has grown and changed dramatically just during the time I've been involved with the city. The town's motto, "Auburn, More than You Imagined," is sometimes considered a joke among some groups of locals who respond with, "Well, that's because you didn't imagine much." Spending time as a pedestrian walking throughout Auburn and its parks, slowing down to the pace of steps and the rhythm of walking, I have come to see the town as more than I imagined, as well.

I find myself wondering, "How I can make my walks and journeys around Auburn more like Mayer's journey through Lenox?" I wonder which famous people herald from Auburn? I suspect it wouldn't be nearly as illustrious of a group as Mayer's list. I could do research about the early uses of the parks I walk through. One park was formerly the location of a mill. What did they mill there? Another park was a location where the State Game Department raised game birds for hunting. The Interurban Trail was built on what used to be the railway for the Interurban Trolley that connected Tacoma, Seattle, and Everett during my grandmother's day. The Environmental Park used to be a hops farm. Perhaps if I research the specific history of places around town, it will provide me with further food for ruminations while walking.

I felt inspired after reading Perec to consider a future project where I station myself at some spot in Auburn and observe the comings and goings with the cataloging details of Perec. My walks through the local parks have so far been movement through space, but now I wonder how the park would differ if I were stationary and the park's inhabitants and visitors sauntered past me, instead.

My own walks in Auburn have helped me realize how much I actually do know about the local community and the history of Auburn, from the town's original name, Slaughter, to its function as a farming community for Japanese immigrants, through Auburn's time when it was a hub for the railroad, to today's bustling outlet mall, racetrack, casino, and Bingo hall. By doing further research into the city's history, by experimenting with different ways of experiencing Auburn (walking, stationery viewing, driving, biking, etc.), and by playing with a variety of forms (prose poetry, tankas, prose, descriptions, reflections) to express my experiences, I believe it may be possible to communicate to a reader the everyday quotidian details of life in Auburn as well as presenting its rich history in clear and entertaining ways.

Bibliography

Alys, Francis. "Interview" (with Russell Ferguson),
    Francis Alys, ed. Cuauhtemoc Medina.
    London: Phaidon, 2007.

Fitch, Andy. *Sixty Morning Walks*. Brooklyn, NY:
    Ugly Duckling Presse, 2014.

Hirsch, Edward. "My Pace Provokes My Thoughts:
    Poetry and Walking." *The American
    Poetry Review* 40.2 (2011): 5-11. JSTOR.
    Web. 28 Feb. 2015.

Jacks, Ben. "Reimagining Walking: Four
    Practices." *Journal of Architectural Education*
    (1984-) 57.3 (2004): 5-9. JSTOR. Web. 1 Mar.
    2015.

Mayer, Bernadette. *Midwinter Day*. New York, NY:
    New Directions Corporation, 1999.

Mullen, Harryette Romell. *Urban Tumbleweed: Notes
    from a Tanka Diary*. Minneapolis: Graywolf,
    2013. Print.

Perec, Georges, and trans. Marc Lowenthal. *An
    Attempt at Exhausting a Place in Paris*.
    Cambridge, MA: Wakefield, 2010.

Phillips, Siobhan. "Wallace Stevens and the Mode of
    the Ordinary." *Twentieth Century Literature* 4.1 (Spring
    2008): 1-30. JSTOR. Web. 28 Feb. 2015.

Thoreau, Henry David. *Walking*. Place of publication
    not identified: [publisher not identified],1999.

About the Author

Deborah Taylor-Hough—long-time Auburn, Washington resident—raised her children in this quaint and growing community. Her family spent many idyllic days walking Auburn's parks throughout the years. Debi is the author of several popular books including *Frugal Living for Dummies®* (Wiley) and the bestselling *Frozen Assets* cookbook series (SourceBooks). Debi received a Master in Fine Arts in Creative Writing and Poetics from the University of Washington Bothell, and is an alumna of the University of Washington Tacoma.

Other Works by This Author

Poetry/Prose

> *A[not]her Nature*
> *Bad Things Happen: An Erasure*

Chapbooks

> *Proverbia*
> *Midwinter Experiments*
> *The UnSilencing*

Nonfiction

> *Frugal Living for Dummies*®
> *Frozen Assets*
> *Frozen Assets Lite & Easy*
> *A Simple Choice*
> *A Twaddle-Free Education*
> *Mix-n-Match Recipes*
> *The Original Simple Mom's Idea Book*
> *Simple Living*

Colophon

Walking Auburn Parks was originally written as a chapbook-style collection of journal writings and black-and-white photography completed by Deborah Taylor-Hough during the 2015 Winter Quarter of the Master of Fine Arts (MFA) in Creative Writing & Poetics at the University of Washington Bothell.

All photos were shot with a camera on a personal cell phone. *Walking Auburn Parks* was written, typed, and formatted on a personal Dell laptop computer using Microsoft Word and a 11-point Garamond font.